monday morning®

Animals

WRITING
AND READING
ACTIVITIES AND PATTERNS

By Victoria Ingram

Publisher: Roberta Suid
Editor: Mary McClellan
Design: Susan Pinkerton
Cover Design: David Hale
Cover Art: Corbin Hillam
Art: Philip Chalk

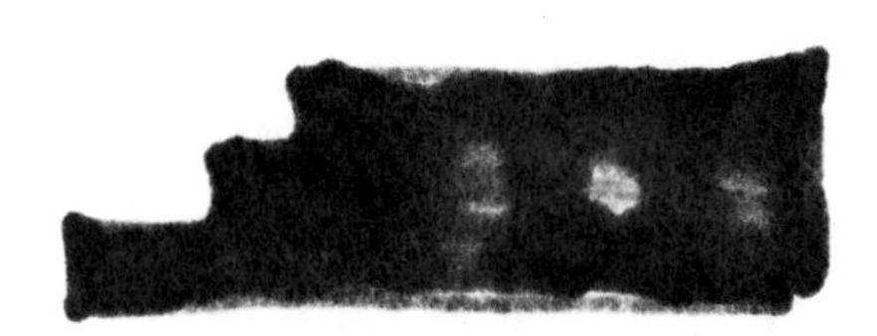

monday morning®

Monday Morning is a registered trademark
of Monday Morning Books, Inc.

ISBN 0–912107–61–8

Printed in the United States of America

9 8 7 6 5 4 3 2 1

INTRODUCTION

This *Language Arts and Crafts* book offers primary-grades teachers fun, classroom-tested projects that motivate creative writing and promote the love of reading. The projects help students to develop perceptual and motor skills, as well as encourage verbal and written expression. In addition, each project incorporates students' own creative ideas, inviting them to use their imaginations.

Each project includes a list of the materials needed and step-by-step instructions for assembly. Materials listed are readily available and assembly is easy. Students learn sequencing as they follow the directions to create these fun and friendly characters. Encourage students to pick their own colors of construction paper and to add their own touches to make their projects special.

A "Related Reading" list is provided for each project, suggesting a variety of books, poems, and songs to be shared with the class. "Story Starters" offer ideas and questions for students to create their own "make-believe" or "fact" stories about the characters they have made. Kindergarten students can "dictate" their stories for you to write down, or they can compose a story as a class as you write it on the chalkboard.

"Follow-Through Activities" are provided for each project to help you plan related study units, field trips, and games.

Creative writing and language activities will take on another dimension as students create their artwork and relate their creations to the language experience.

Tips

1. You can make tagboard patterns for most pattern pieces. Students then trace around the tagboard patterns and cut out the pieces. You can make ditto masters for the more detailed pieces—especially for younger children—or to save time. Run the ditto masters off on colored paper, and have the children cut out the pieces.
2. For best results, make each project ahead of time as a sample for the class. This sample is useful for demonstrating how to assemble the project.
3. Show students how to fold paper and trace a pattern so that it can be cut to produce two identical pieces (eyes, hands, boots, etc.).
4. As a general rule, the head is glued onto the front of the neck, and hands are glued to the back of the arms.
5. A buckle can be made easily by folding a rectangle in half, and then drawing a border around three sides, leaving the folded side without a border.
6. Use red chalk to color cheeks. Apply the chalk, and then have students rub it in with a circular motion to blend the color into the cheeks.

7. Some students may be more motivated to write a story before the project is assembled. They can then look forward to the project as a reward.
8. Relate the project and the language activities to something you are studying in class. Use the related reading materials for enrichment.
9. Always encourage creativity and allow differences for each project. Each student's effort should have its own special look. Display the finished projects with the creative writing for everyone to enjoy. Parents love to see what their children have done when they visit for open house.

Resource Materials

Books Kids Will Sit Still For, Judy Freeman. Alleyside Press, 1984

This book offers helpful information on books to read aloud to young children.

Children's Writing, Leonard Sealey, Nancy Sealey, and Marcia Millmore. International Reading Association, 1979

This is an excellent resource for teachers who teach writing. Topics covered are "The Rationale for Writing in Primary Grades," "Generating Writing by Young Children," "A Structured Approach to Writing for Young Children," "Some Practical Aspects," and "Writing Activities."

The Random House Book of Fairy Tales, adapted by Amy Ehrlich. Random House, 1985

A good collection of fairy tales to be used as related reading.

The Random House Book of Poetry, selected by Jack Prelutsky. Random House, 1983

A helpful anthology of poetry for young children. All poems listed in "Related Reading" are found in this book unless otherwise noted.

The Read-Aloud Handbook, Jim Trelease. Penguin Books, 1985

A very useful book on the art of reading aloud. It offers suggestions on how to read aloud effectively to various age groups and gives an annotated bibliography of good "read-aloud" books.

Winter Wonders, Toni Bauman and June Zinkgraf. Good Apple, 1978

This book offers fun projects to be used as "Follow-Through Activities." It is especially helpful to use with the lion, the mouse, and the penguin.

LION

Materials

Construction paper:

white or yellow for mane, paws, and mouth

brown for face, ears, and legs

pink scrap for inner ears

black scrap for eyes and nose

Scissors, glue, crayons or markers

Construction

1. Make ditto masters for mane, paws, mouth, face, and ears.
2. Cut out all pieces.
3. Trace lines on mane and paws with black or brown crayon.
4. Glue head to center of mane and ears to back head.
5. Glue paws to front of legs and then glue legs to back of mane.
6. Glue mouth to face, letting chin hang over bottom edge.
7. Cut freehand eyes, nose, and inner ears. Glue into place. Eyes should be right above cheeks.
8. Using a black crayon or marker, make whiskers and eyebrows or eyelashes.
9. Color tongue red.

Related Reading

Brown, Margaret Wise. *The Sleepy Little Lion.* Harper & Row, 1976
Fatio, Louise. *The Happy Lion* and *The Happy Lioness.* McGraw-Hill, 1964, 1980
Hamsa, Bobbie. *Your Pet Lion.* Childrens, 1981
Sendak, Maurice. *Pierre.* Harper & Row, 1962
POEM: "Lion" by William Jay Smith

Story Starters

Read *The Sleepy Little Lion* to the students. Then ask students, "Can you remember what the sleepy little lion did in the story? Write as many things as you can remember." This is also a good opportunity to practice sequence.

Read *Your Pet Lion.* "Write a silly story about your lion pet. Give your lion a name."

Read *Dandelion* to the students and discuss the story. Then ask students to write about the moral of the story: "Is it better to be yourself?"

Follow-Through Activities

This project would complement a unit study about zoo animals. Children could write stories about a visit to the zoo and make the lion to display with their stories.

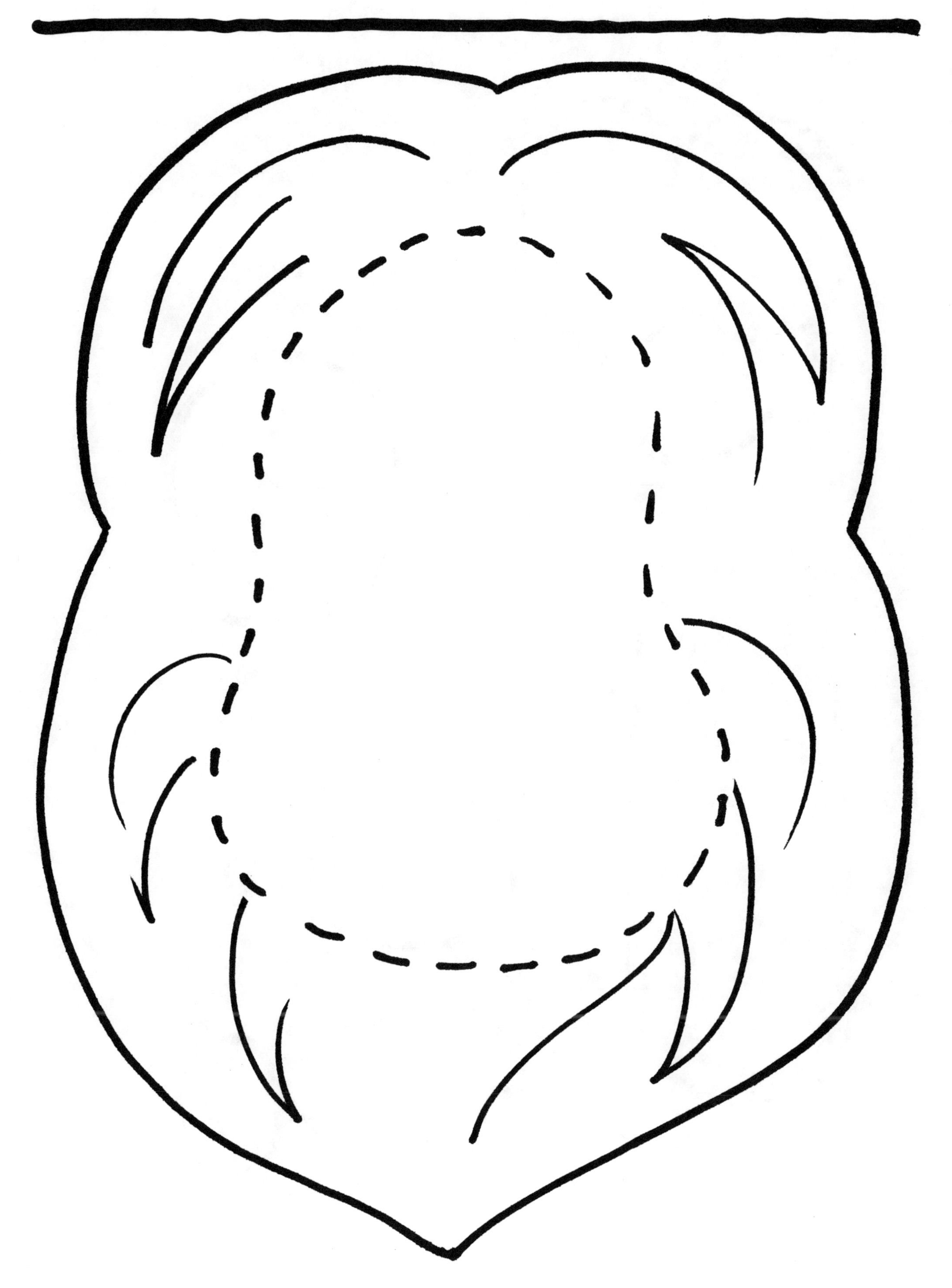

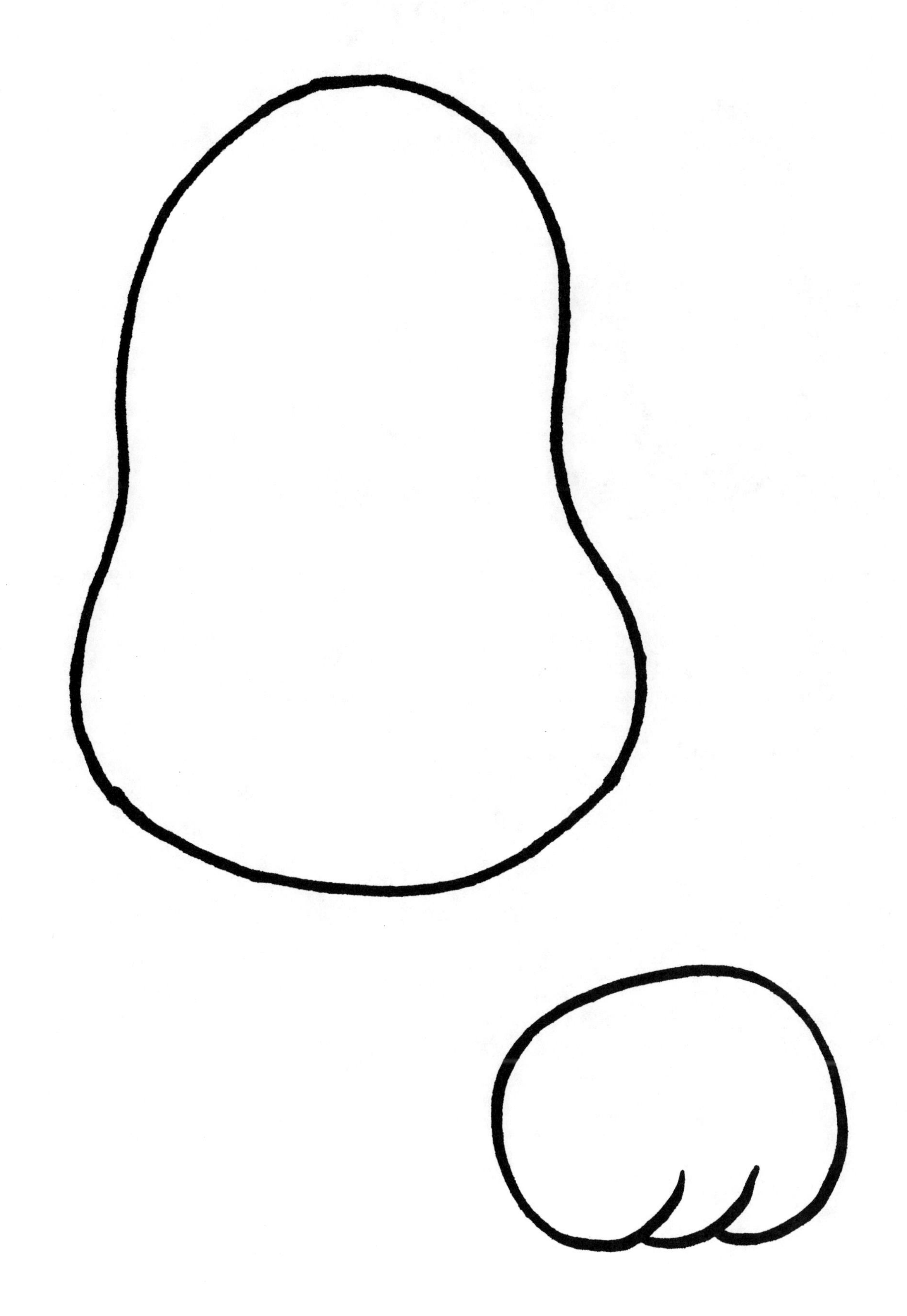

PENGUIN

Materials

Construction paper:
- black for body and eyes
- orange for feet and nose
- white for stomach

Scissors, glue

Construction

1. Make tagboard patterns for body, stomach, and feet.
2. Trace patterns and cut them out.
3. Cut eyes and nose freehand.
4. Glue stomach onto front of body.
5. Glue feet to back of body, facing out.
6. Glue eyes and nose onto face.

Related Reading

Brenner, Barbara. *Walt Disney's The Penguin That Hated the Cold.* Random, 1973

Freeman, Don. *Penguins, Of All People.* Viking, 1971

Hamsa, Bobbie. *Your Pet Penguin.* Childrens, 1980

Hogan, Paula Z. *Penguin.* Raintree Pubs., 1979

Lepthien, Emilie U. *Penguins.* Childrens, 1983

Serventy, Vincent. *Animals in the Wild: Penguin.* Scholastic, 1983

Story Starters

After the class has learned about penguins and where they live, ask the students to write a fact story telling something interesting and true that they have learned. "Where do penguins live? What kind of animal are they? Can they fly? How are their babies born and what do they eat?"

Read *Your Pet Penguin* to the students and then have them write a silly story about a pet penguin. "Pretend that you have a pet penguin. Where would your penguin sleep? What would you feed your penguin?"

Follow-Through Activities

Use this project as a part of a unit on Antarctica. This will help dispel the notion that penguins live at the North Pole.

Penguins are also easily adapted to a unit on birds or on weather.

TIGER

Materials

Construction paper:

orange for head, ears, legs, and body
white for mouth and inner ears
black scraps for nose and eyes

Scissors, glue, black crayons or markers

Construction

1. Make ditto masters for patterns.
2. Cut out all pieces.
3. Glue head to top of body.
4. Glue inner ears to ears and then glue ears to back of head.
5. Glue mouth to face.
6. Cut eyes and nose freehand and glue into place. (Eyes may also be drawn)
7. Draw tiger stripes with markers or crayons. Make whiskers and eyelashes.

Related Reading

Hogan, Paula Z. *Tiger.* Raintree Pubs., 1979
Kraus, Robert. *Leo the Late Bloomer.* Crowell, 1971
Oetting, Rae. *Timmy Tiger* Series. Oddo, 1981
Pinkwater, Honest Dan'l. *Roger's Umbrella.* Dutton, 1982
Zolotow, Charlotte. *Tiger Called Thomas.* Lothrop, 1963

Story Starters

After reading *Leo the Late Bloomer*, discuss how people progress at their own rates. "What is a late bloomer?" "Can you think of something that took you a long time to learn but made you very happy when you finally did?" "Is it okay if some things take people longer to learn?"

Write an adventure story about Timmy the Tiger after reading some of his stories.

Write a fact story about tigers after studying about them.

Follow-Through Activities

After reading *Roger's Umbrella*, display an umbrella in the classroom where everyone can see and use it. Write some sentences for the children to act out, one at a time, while other students try to guess what is being acted out. Put the sentences on small cards and let students have fun drawing and acting. Sentences should involve the umbrella. Examples: "The umbrella is spinning like a top." "The umbrella is floating on the water." "The umbrella is rolling like a wheel."

PUPPY

Materials

Construction paper:
- brown, yellow, white, or gray for body, head, ears, foot, and tail
- white for mouth
- black scraps for eyes and nose

Yarn for bow (optional)
Correction fluid (optional)
Scissors, glue, crayons or markers

Construction

1. Make ditto masters for patterns.
2. Trace lines and color spots before cutting pieces.
3. Cut out all pieces.
4. Glue head to straight side of dog's body.
5. Glue mouth onto lower edge of head, letting mouth hang over bottom edge.
6. Glue foot behind head to right of dog's mouth.
7. Glue ears to top sides of head.
8. Cut freehand eyes, nose, and tail. Glue into place. Eyes sit right over top edge of cheeks. Cut large eyes from a folded piece of paper. Cut tiny white circles for insides of eyes or use correction fluid to make dots on eyes. (Teacher should apply fluid if used.)
9. Glue tail to back of dog and place a yarn bow on tail.

Related Reading

Gackenbach, Dick. *A Bag Full of Pups* and *Claude the Dog.* Houghton Mifflin, 1983, 1982

Hurd, Thacher. *Hobo Dog* and *Hobo Dog's Christmas Tree.* Scholastic, 1981, 1983

Kellogg, Steven. *Penkerton, Behave.* Dial, 1982

Selsam, Millicent E. *How Puppies Grow.* Scholastic, 1972

POEMS: "The Hairy Dog" by Herbert Asquith
"Roger the Dog" by Ted Hughes
"Lone Dog" by Irene McLeod
"Mother Doesn't Want a Dog" by Judith Viorst
"My Dog" by Marchette Chute from *Around and About.* Economy, 1967

SONGS: "Bingo" from *Eye Winker, Tom Tinker, Chin Chopper*
"How Much Is That Doggie in the Window?" by Bob Merrill
"Oh Where Has My Little Dog Gone?" from *Mickey's Favorite Children's Songs*

Story Starters

After reading *A Bag Full of Pups,* ask students to write a story about the puppy that was the last to find a home. "Pretend that you are the little boy at the end of the story and tell what you would do with your new puppy. Give your puppy a name."

"Write a story about your own dog. What's your dog's name? Tell something funny that the dog has done or even something bad. If you don't have a dog, write about a neighbor's dog and what you have seen the dog do. Or make up a story about the dog you would like to have someday."

Follow-Through Activities

Have students write as many words as they can think of that rhyme with *dog.* Make a bulletin board displaying the dogs and the rhyming words. Or display the dogs along with the stories for everyone to enjoy.

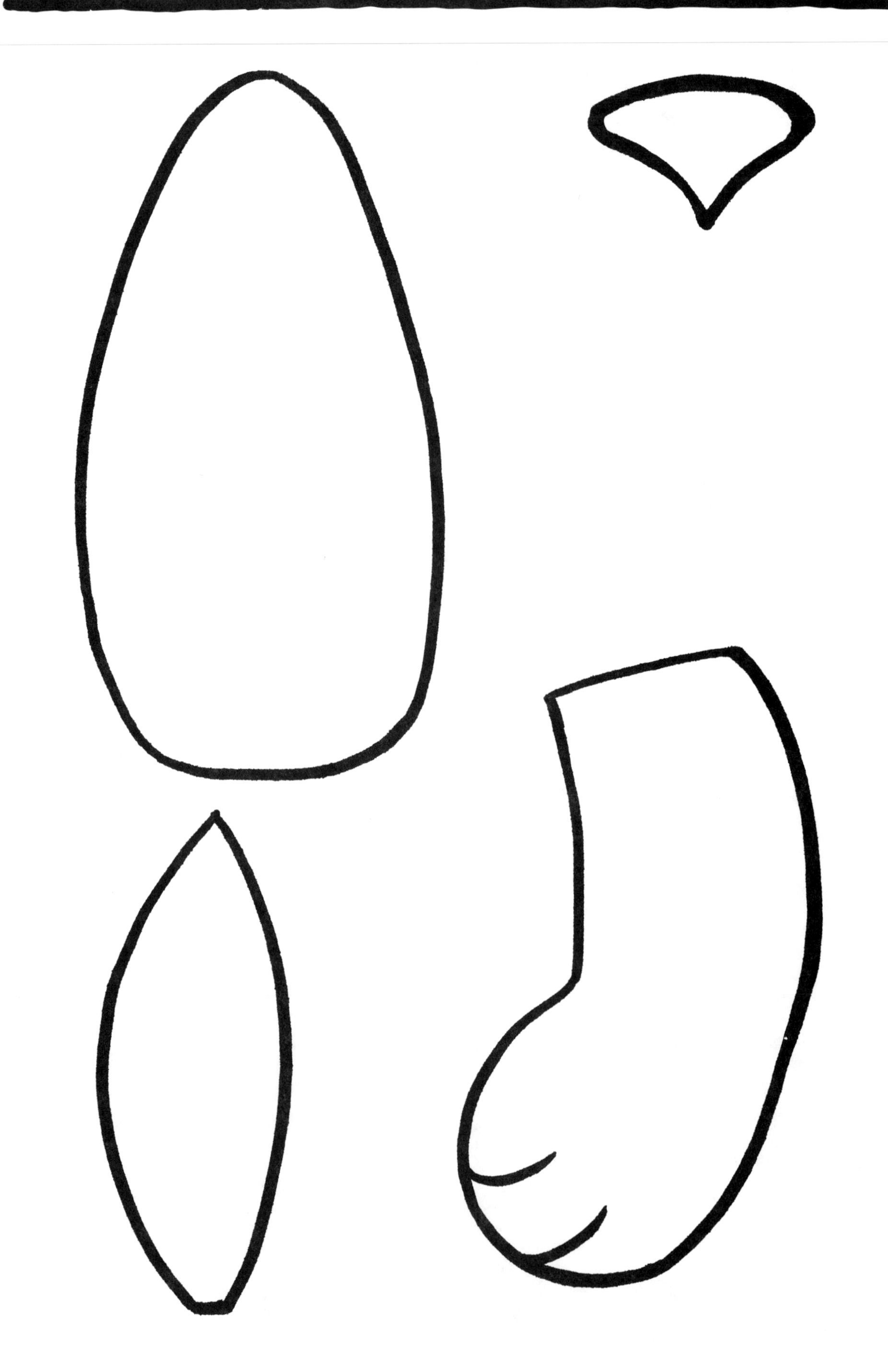

GIRAFFE

Materials

Construction paper:
- yellow for head, ears, neck, body, and legs
- brown for mane, tail, and spots
- orange for horns

Brown yarn for hair (optional)

Scissors, glue, crayons or markers, orange chalk

Note: The giraffe is nearly three-feet tall when finished.

Construction

1. Make ditto masters and run off patterns for all pieces except horns. Horns can be made from tagboard patterns.
2. Trace horns and cut them out.
3. Cut out all other pattern pieces.
4. Glue legs (one piece) to back of body.
5. Glue neck to back of body. Glue tail to back of body.
6. Glue ears and horns to back of head and then glue head to front of neck.
7. Eyes can be drawn with black crayon or marker or cut from black and white scraps. Draw mouth and nose. Use orange chalk for cheeks.
8. Students can have fun cutting spots freehand and gluing them to the giraffe.
9. Cut a few strands of brown yarn and glue to head.

Related Reading

Brenner, Barbara. *Mr. Tall and Mr. Small.* Random, 1980
Brown, Louise C. *Giraffes.* Dodd, 1980
Cooke, Ann. *Giraffes at Home.* Harper & Row, 1972
Duvoisin, Roger. *Periwinkle.* Knopf, 1976
Hamsa, Bobbie. *Your Pet Giraffe.* Childrens, 1982
Rey, H.A. *Cecily G. and the Nine Monkeys.* Houghton Mifflin, 1977
Silverstein, Shel. *A Giraffe and a Half.* Harper & Row, 1964

Story Starters

Read *Mr. Tall and Mr. Small* to the children. Then discuss the advantages and disadvantages of being as big as a giraffe or as small as a mouse. Make the mouse project that follows this one. Students can pick one to write about. "I would rather be a giraffe because . . ."

"Write a fact story about giraffes after learning all about them. Relate as many true facts as you can about a giraffe." Example: Giraffes are the tallest animals on earth.

Follow-Through Activities

Display the giraffe in the hallway along with the mouse. Make a sign that says "Mr. Tall and Mr. Small."

Study the giraffe and other zoo animals. Take a trip to the zoo if possible.

Read *A Giraffe and a Half* and have students recall the sequence. This is also an excellent source for fun with rhyming words.

Relate this project to the study of the soft *g* sound. Have students find other words with the soft *g* sound and display the words in a learning center.

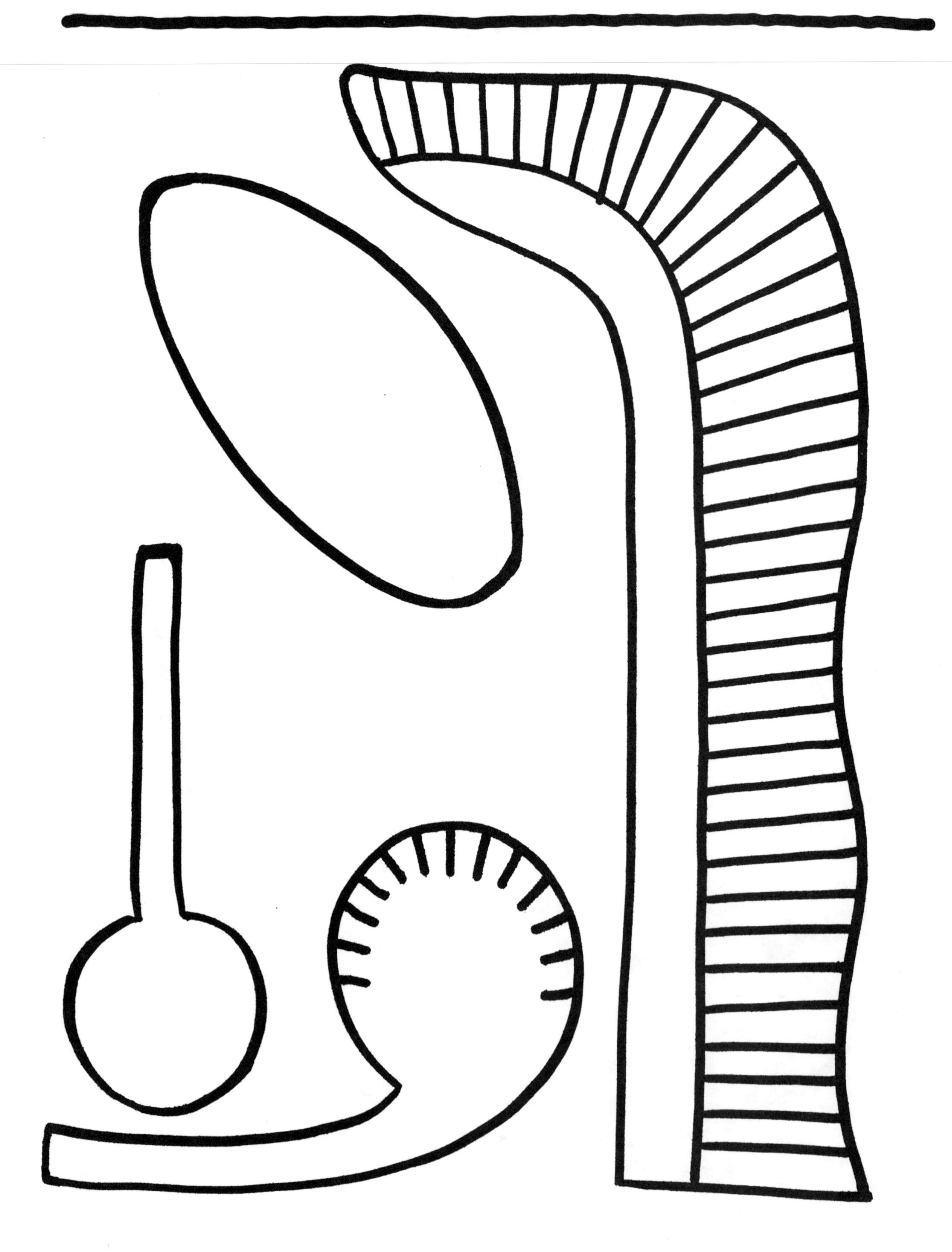

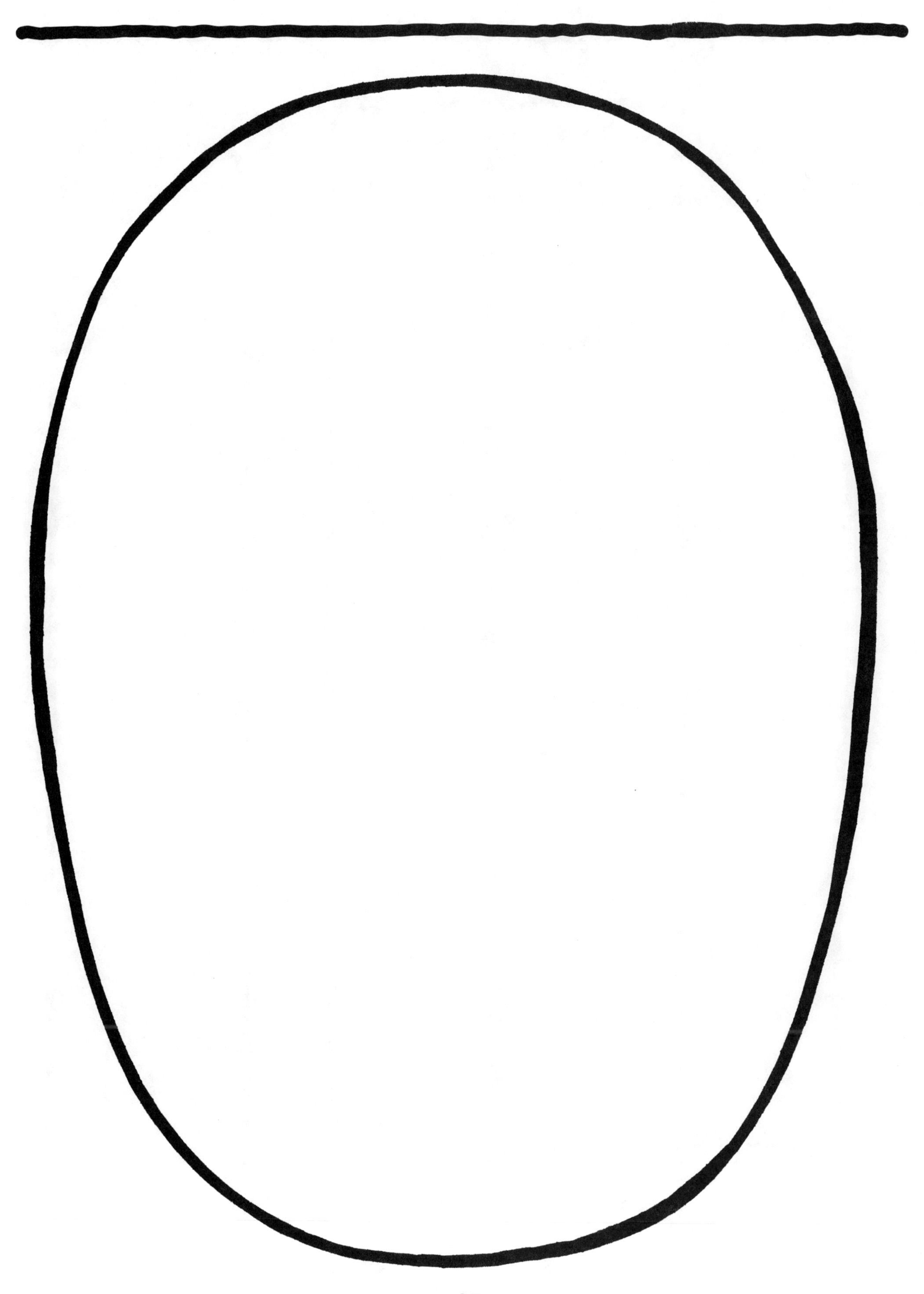

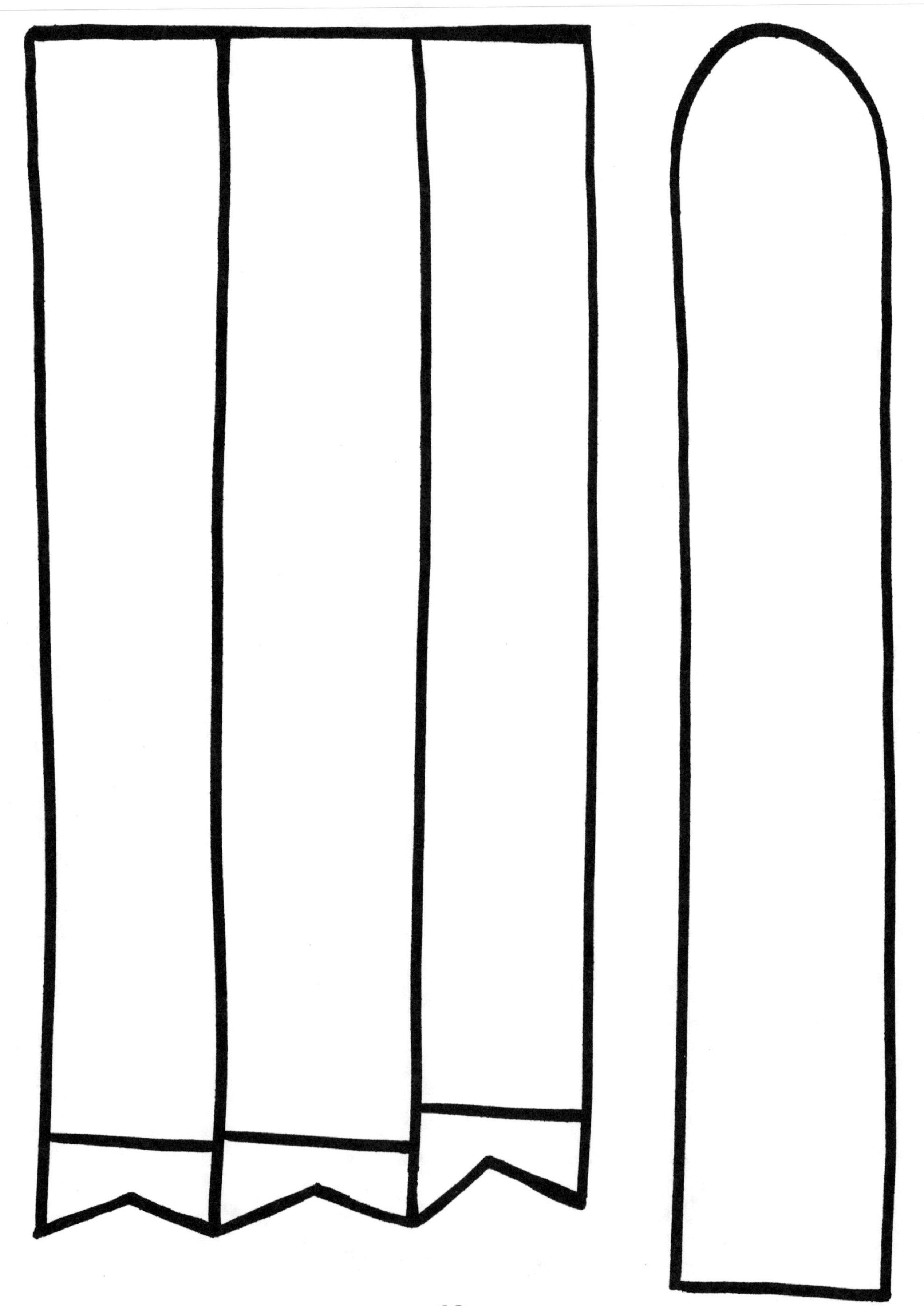

MOUSE

Materials

Construction paper:
- blue or gray for body, head, and ears
- pink for inner ears
- white for eyes, tummy, and mouth

Black or blue pipe cleaner for tail

Cotton for head (optional)

Scissors, glue, black crayons or markers, red chalk

Construction

1. Cut out all pieces.
2. Glue head to front of neck. Make sure pointed edge is up for top of head.
3. Glue pink inner ears to larger outer ears. Then glue ears to back of head.
4. Using a black crayon or marker, fill in four feet. Trace arm and leg lines.
5. Glue tummy to body.
6. Glue mouth piece to lower edge of face. Then add black and white ovals cut freehand for eyes. Nose can be cut freehand and glued over mouth. Use chalk for cheeks.
7. Draw black whiskers with pen or marker and add eyelashes.
8. Tape pipe cleaner to back and shape with curves.
9. Add dab of white cotton to top of head.

Related Reading

Cosgrove, Stephen. *Little Mouse on the Prairie.* Price Stern, 1978
Gackenbach, Dick. *The Perfect Mouse.* Macmillan, 1984
Houston, John. *A Mouse in My House.* Random, 1980
Kraus, Robert. *Whose Mouse Are You?* Macmillan, 1972
Lobel, Arnold. *Mouse Soup.* Harper & Row, 1977
McNulty, Faith. *Mouse and Tim.* Harper & Row, 1978
POEMS: "Mice" by Rose Fyleman
"The Waltzer in the House" by Stanley Kunitz

Story Starters

Read *Mouse and Tim* and talk about what it would be like to be a mouse. "Where could you go? What would you do? What would you eat?" Begin creative writing with: "If I were a mouse . . ."

Being as tiny as a mouse can create many problems. Have the students think of and name as many problems as they can. Examples: A mouse can't open a door or ride a bike. A mouse must watch out for cars and cats!

Read the poem "Mice" and then ask students, "Why do you think mice are nice?"

Follow-Through Activities

Memorize the poem "Mice" and give special recognition to those who can recite it.

This project can also be related to the special sound *ou.*

Older children can write poems about a mouse.

Display finished mice along with writing or reward children when they have memorized the poem by letting them take their mice home.

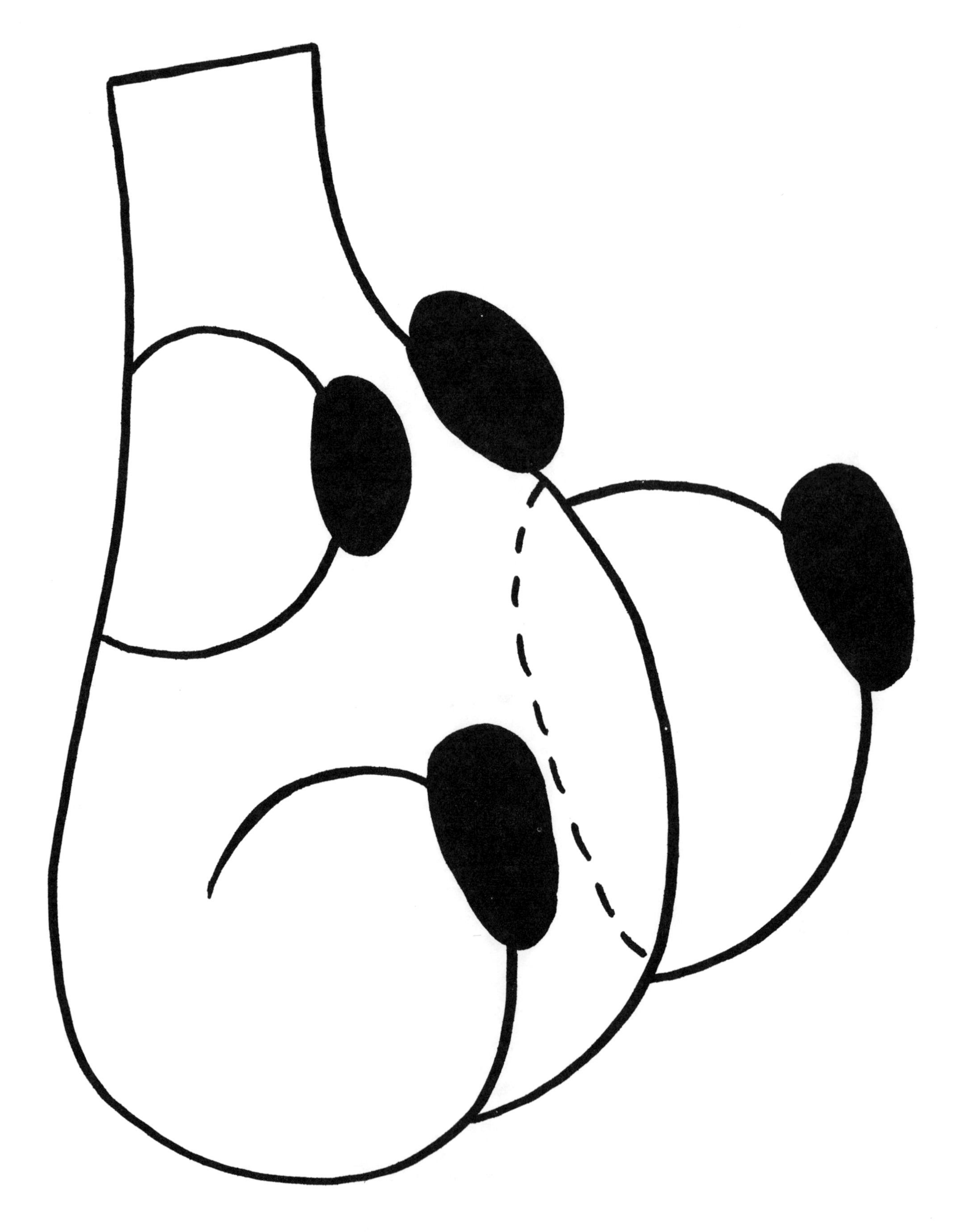

MONKEY

Materials
Construction paper:
brown for head, body, ears, arms, and tail
pink or manila for face and tummy
Scissors, glue, crayons or markers

Construction
1. Cut out all pieces.
2. Glue arms to back of body. Glue tail to back.
3. Glue ears to back of head and tummy to front of body.
4. Glue face to head. Draw eyes, nose, and mouth with crayons or markers.

Eyes can also be cut out of black and white scraps.

Related Reading

Brown, Marc. *The True Francine.* Little, 1981
Fuentes, Vilma M. *Monkey and the Crocodile.* Cellar, 1984
Hoban, Lillian. *Arthur* Series. Harper & Row, 1982–1984
Rey, H.A. and Margaret. *Curious George* Series. Houghton Mifflin, 1973–1984
Slobodkina, Esphyr. *Caps for Sale.* Scholastic, 1984
Whitehead, Patricia. *Monkeys,* Troll Assocs., 1982

Story Starters

Read *The True Francine* to the students and discuss the story. Ask the students to write about an incident they have experienced in school that was unpleasant.

Read the *Curious George* books to the students. Have the students write a curious adventure for Curious George.

Follow-Through Activities

Display the monkeys from a string or piece of yarn across the room. The monkeys can hang by their tails or they can be pinned by their heads or arms.

Monkeys can also be displayed on a bulletin board with a tree as the background. Call it the "Monkey Tree" and have students write silly sentences to be cut into strips and glued to the monkeys.

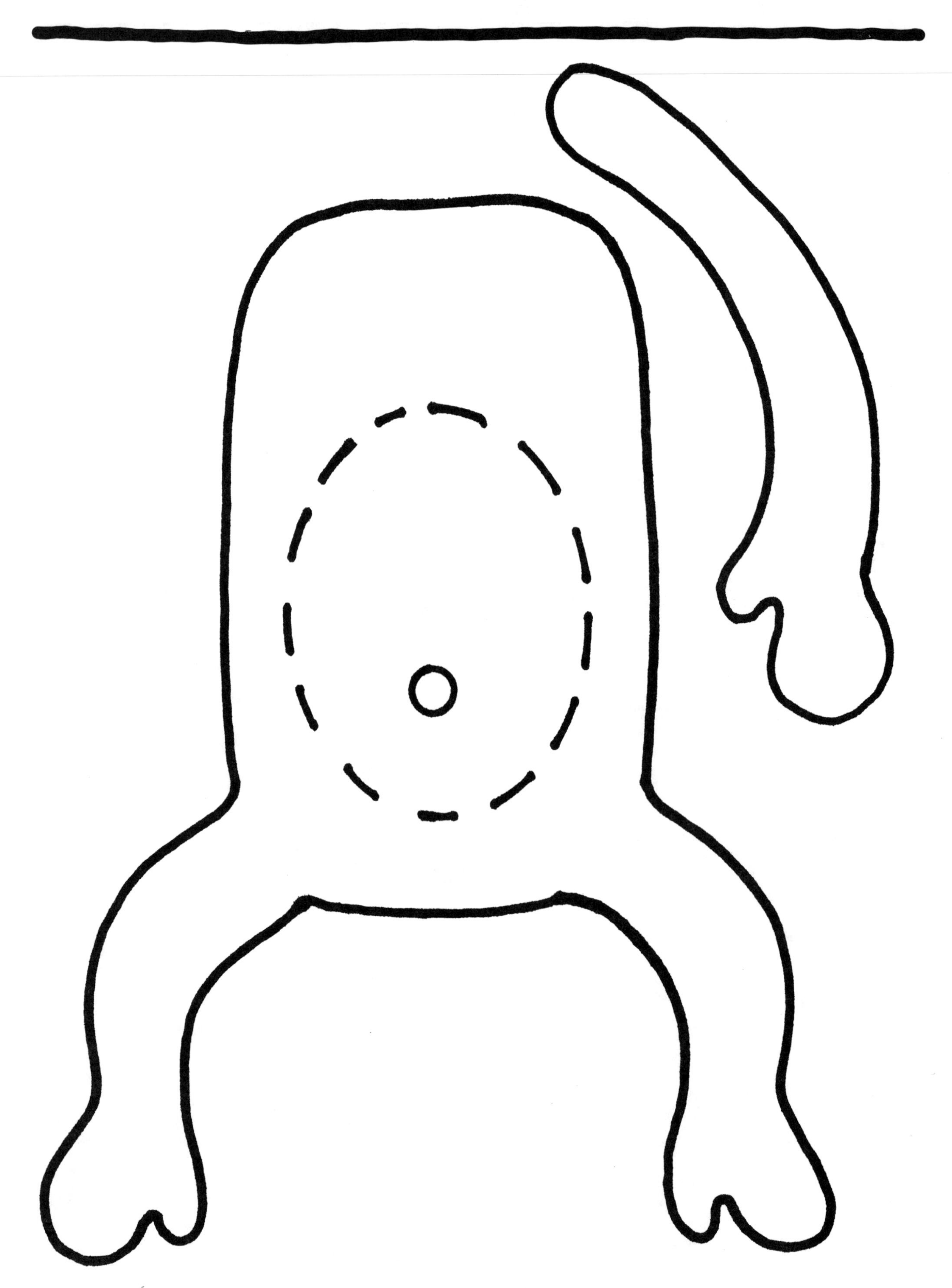

FROG

Materials

Construction paper:

green for head, legs, and body
light green for tummy
black and white scraps for eyes

Scissors, glue, crayons or markers

Construction

1. Cut out all pieces.
2. Glue tummy to body and then glue legs to top of tummy.
3. Glue head to top of body.
4. Cut eyes freehand or draw with marker. Draw mouth and nose.
5. Use a green crayon or marker to make spots on body and face.

Related Reading

Duke, Kate. *Seven Froggies Went to School.* Dutton, 1985
Grimm, Brothers. *The Frog Prince.* Troll Assocs., 1979
Kalan, Robert. *Jump Frog, Jump.* Greenwillow, 1981
Langstaff, John, and Rojankovsky, Feodor. *Frog Went A-Courting.* Harcourt Brace Jovanovich, 1972
Lobel, Arnold. *Frog and Toad.* Harper & Row, 1979
POEMS: "The Tin Frog" by Russell Hoban
"The Toad" by Robert S. Oliver
"The Frog" by Hilaire Belloc
"The Tree Frog" by John Travers Moore
SONG: "Frog Went A-Courting"

Story Starters

After studying about frogs, the students will enjoy writing about what they have learned. "Write as many true facts about frogs as you can remember."

After reading several books about Frog and Toad, students can write a silly story of their own about the characters. Have students share their stories with the class. Make a class book for a reading center.

Follow-Through Activities

Make lily pads and write facts about frogs on them. Display the frogs and the lily pads on a bulletin board for a learning center.

Students can write sentences about real or make-believe frogs and cut sentences into strips to put into a shoe box for a learning center. Mix the strips up. Then have students pull out the strips and tell whether they are about real or make-believe frogs.

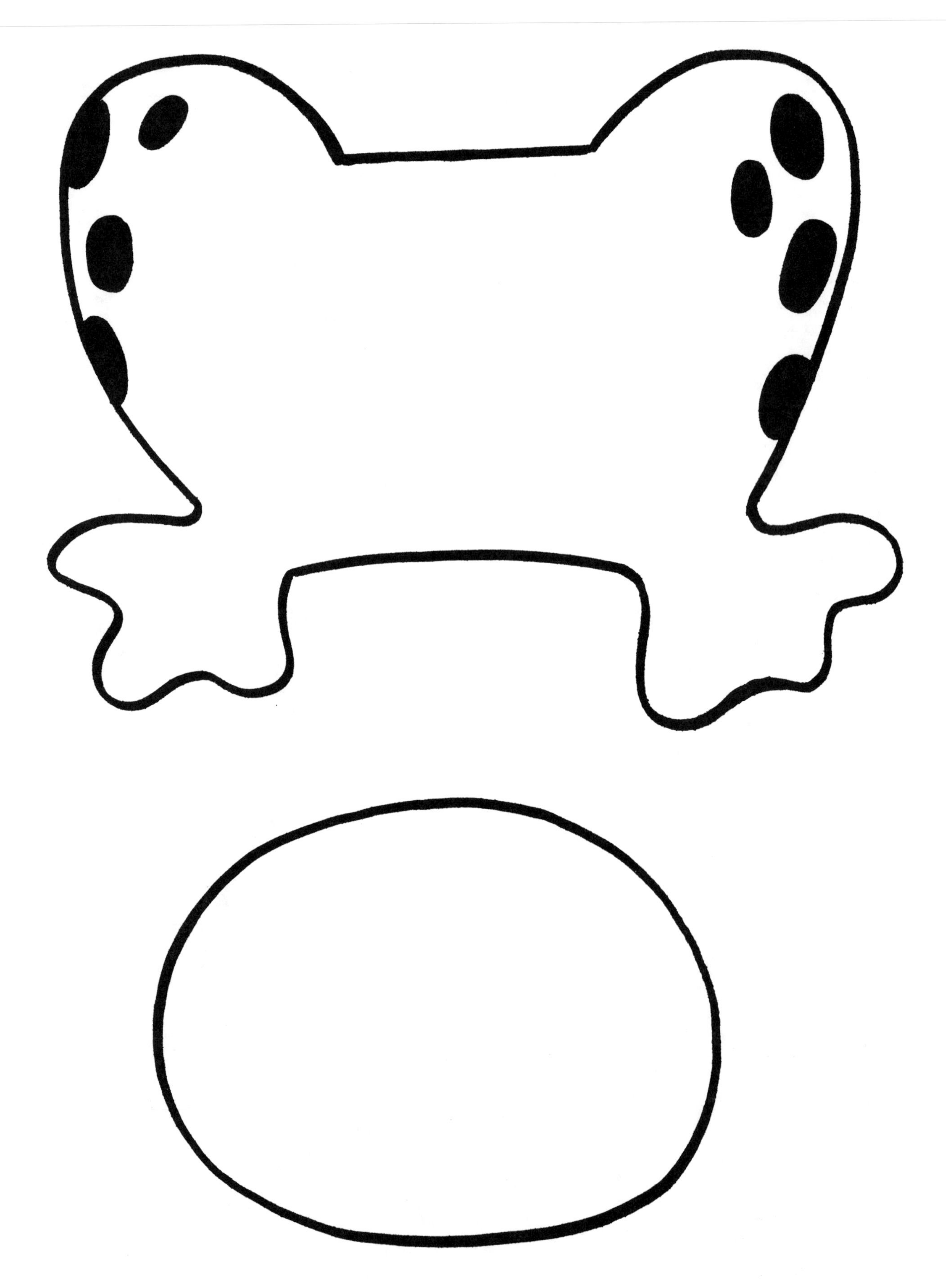

DUCK

Materials
Construction paper:
white for head and body
orange for bill and feet
any color for hat
Scissors, glue, crayons or markers

Construction
1. Cut out all pieces.
2. Eyes can be cut freehand from black scraps or drawn with crayon or marker.
3. Glue feet to back of body. Glue bill to lower half of face, letting mouth hang over bottom edge.
4. Show students how to cut slit in hat for head. Then glue hat in place.

Related Reading

Andersen, Hans Christian. *The Ugly Duckling.* Troll Assocs., 1979
Dunn, Judy. *The Little Duck.* Random, 1976
Flack, Marjorie. *The Story About Ping.* Penguin, 1977
Friskey, Margaret. *Seven Diving Ducks.* Childrens, 1965
McCloskey, Robert. *Make Way for Ducklings.* Penguin, 1976
Roy, Ron. *Three Ducks Went Wandering.* Scholastic, 1980
POEMS: "Ducks' Ditty" by Kenneth Grahame
"The Duck" by Richard Digance
SONGS: "Five Little Ducks" and "The Little White Duck" from Tom Glazer's *Eye Winker, Tom Tinker, Chin Chopper*

Story Starters

"Make up an adventure about a little duck who gets lost." "My duck wears a hat because . . ." "I like ducks because . . ."

Follow-Through Activities

Children will enjoy learning the song "Little White Duck" and then acting out each verse.

This project can easily be made by kindergarten students. Relate this project to the letter *d* or the short vowel sound *u*.

Older students could use this duck for the study of the *ck* sound. Display the duck with a list of the words students have found that contain *ck*.

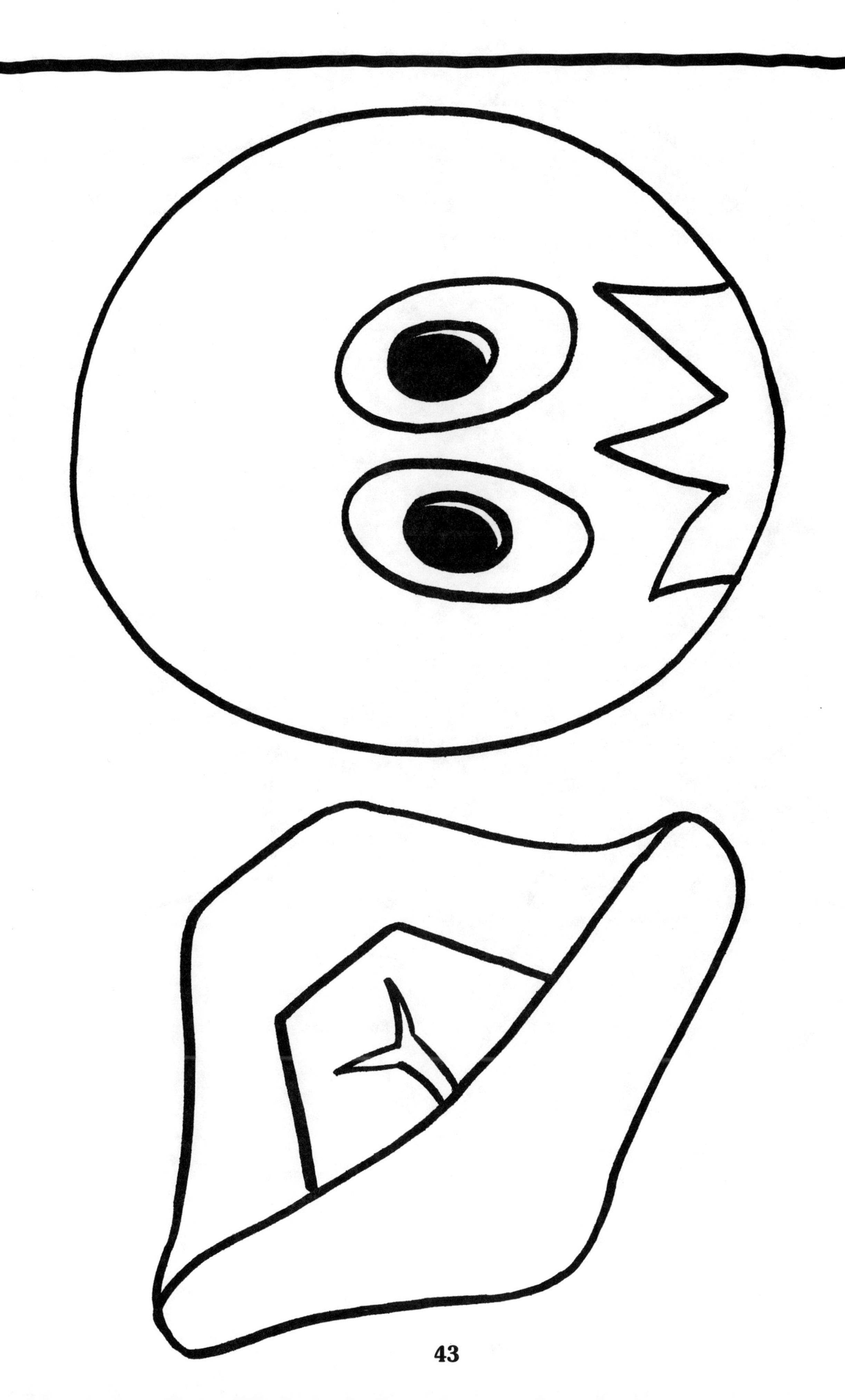

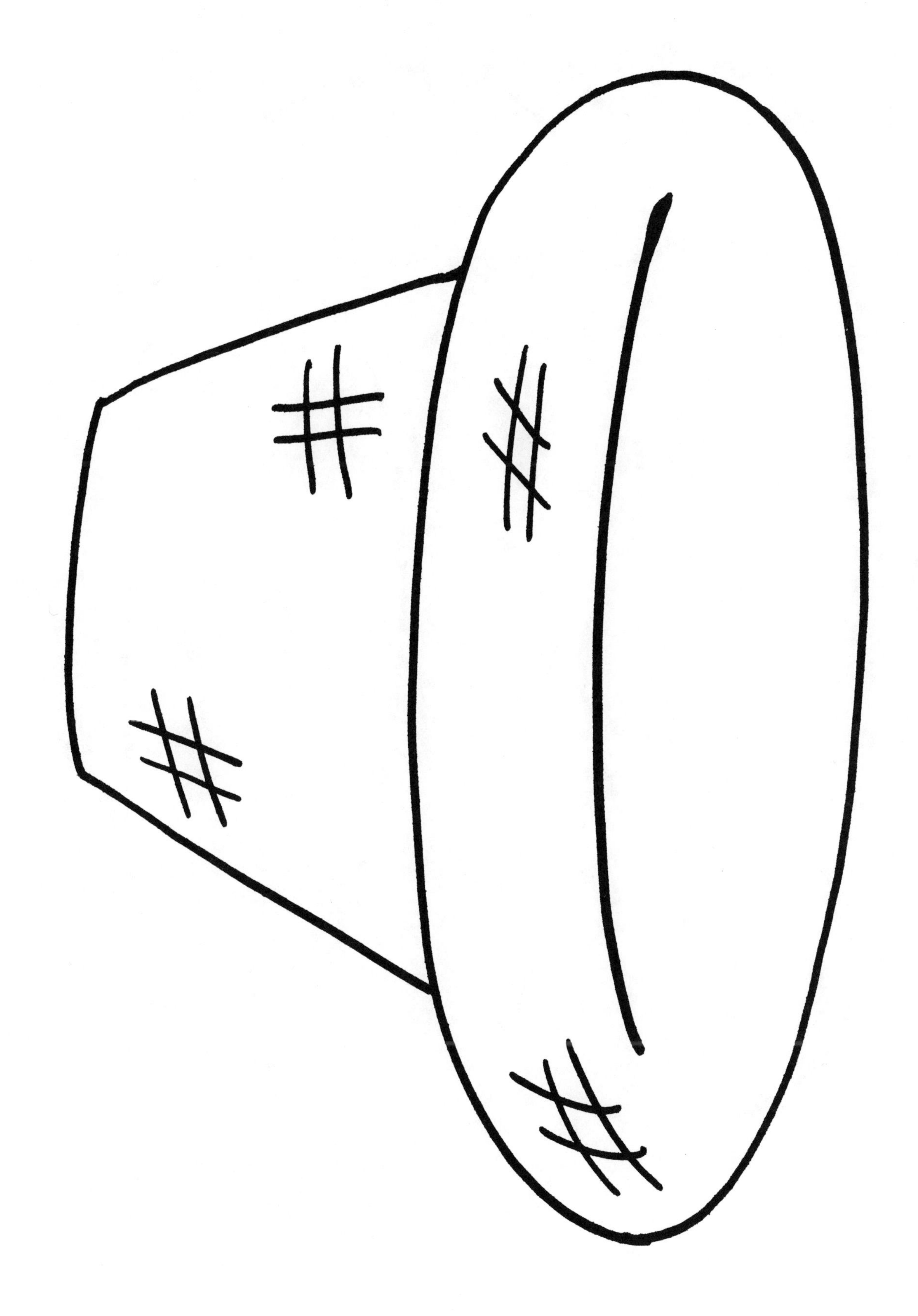

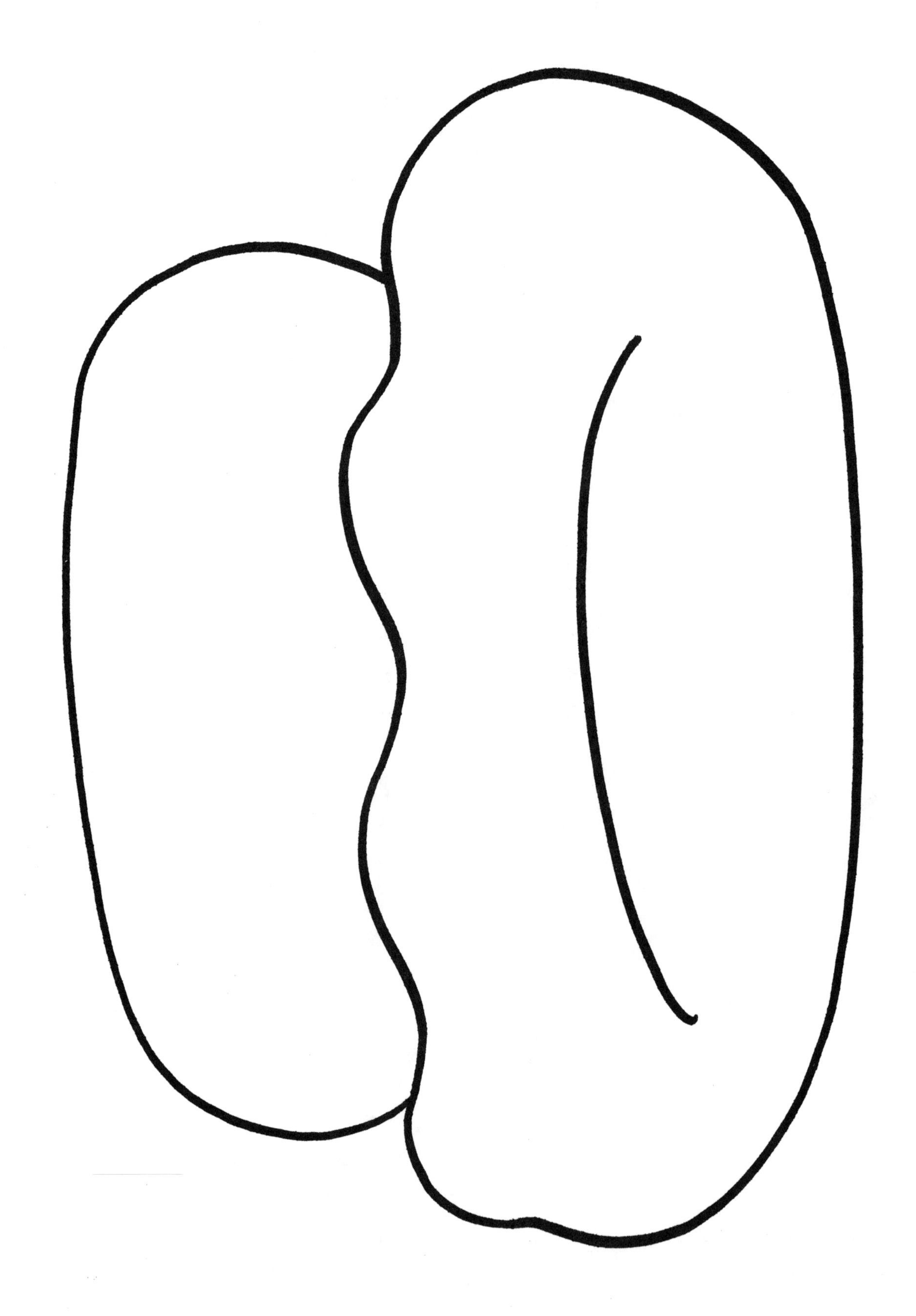

BEAR

Materials

Construction paper:
- brown for body and head
- white or manila for tummy, mouth, and pads
- pink and black scraps for ears, eyes, and nose
- any color for overalls

Buttons (optional)

Scissors, glue, crayons or markers

Construction

1. Cut out all pieces.
2. Glue head to front of neck.
3. Glue mouth onto face.
4. Cut nose and eyes freehand and glue onto face.
5. Cut pink inner ears and glue in center of ears.
6. Use crayons or markers for eyebrows, eyelashes, and dots on cheeks.
7. For body #1, glue on tummy and foot pads. For body #2, glue overalls into place. Tuck straps under head.

Related Reading
Bond, Michael. *Paddington Bear.* Random, 1973
Cauley, Lorinda B. *Goldilocks and the Three Bears.* Putnam Pub. Group, 1981
Freeman, Don. *Corduroy* and *A Pocket for Corduroy.* Penguin, 1976, 1980
Kennedy, Jimmy. *Teddy Bears' Picnic.* Green Tiger, 1983
Rosenthal, Mark. *Bears.* Childrens, 1983
Waber, Bernard. *Ira Sleeps Over.* Houghton Mifflin, 1975
POEM: "Grandpa Bear's Lullaby" by Jane Yolen
SONG: "The Teddy Bears Picnic"

Story Starters
Read *Ira Sleeps Over* and then have students talk about their teddy bears. "Write a story about your teddy bear. Where did you get it? Does your bear sleep with you? What's your bear's name? Would you be embarrassed to take your bear if you were spending the night with a friend?"

Read *Corduroy* and then have students write a make-believe adventure about him. Make the bear with the overalls for this story.

Follow-Through Activities
Present a unit study of bears. Children can write a fact story about what they have learned about bears.

Have a bear party! Pick a special day to have students bring their teddy bears to school. This could be the ending activity of a unit on bears and hibernation. Students may enjoy sharing something special about their bears.

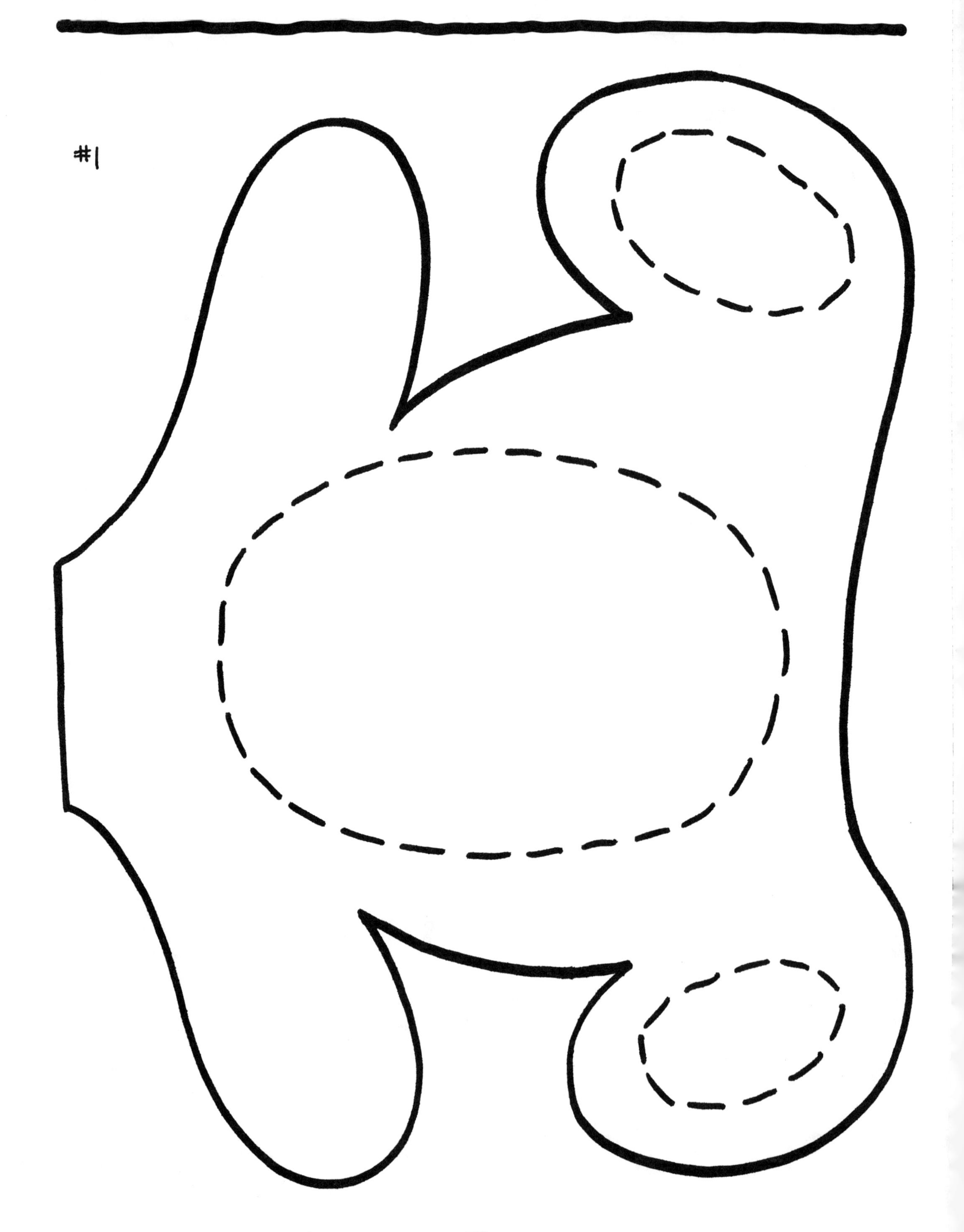
#1

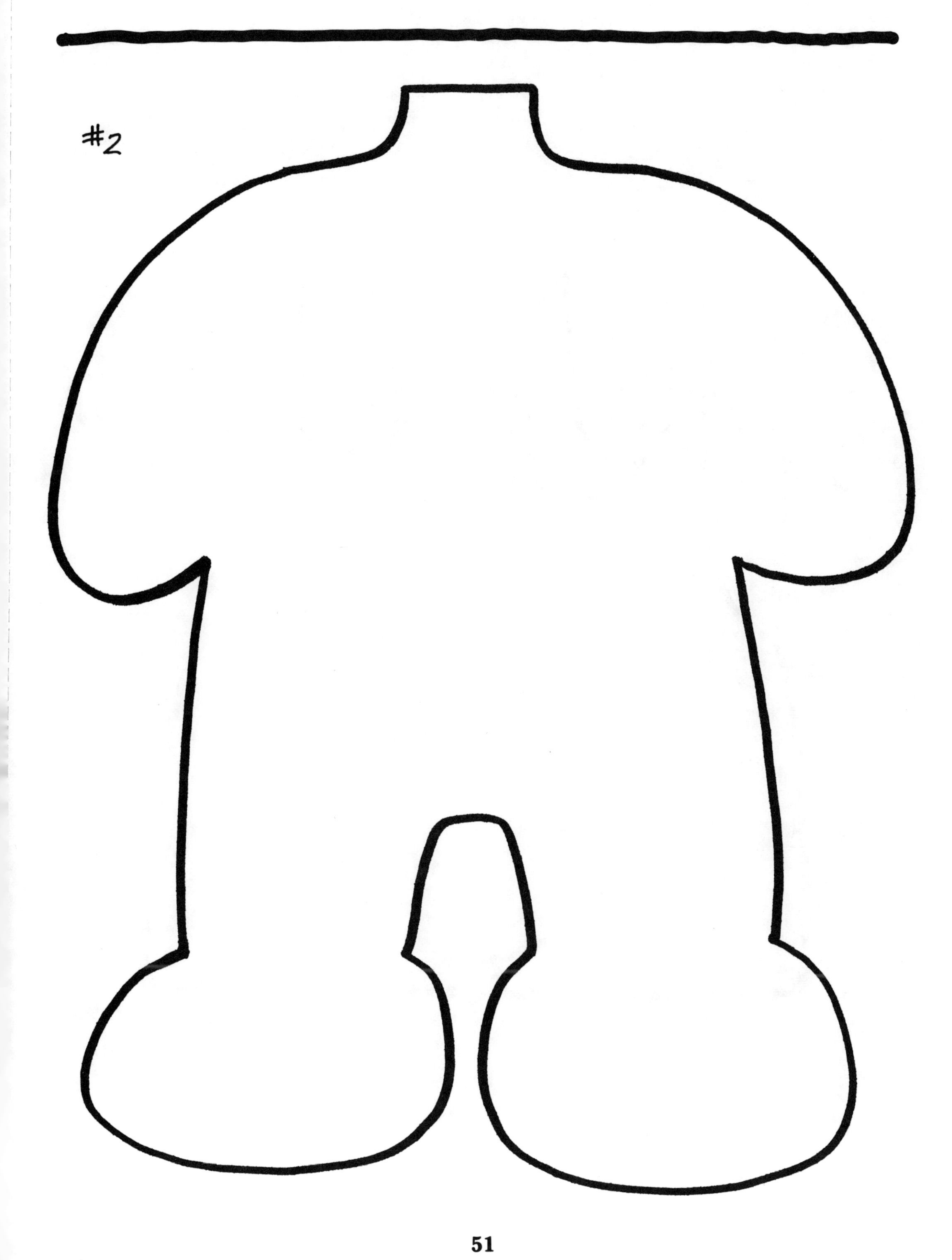
#2

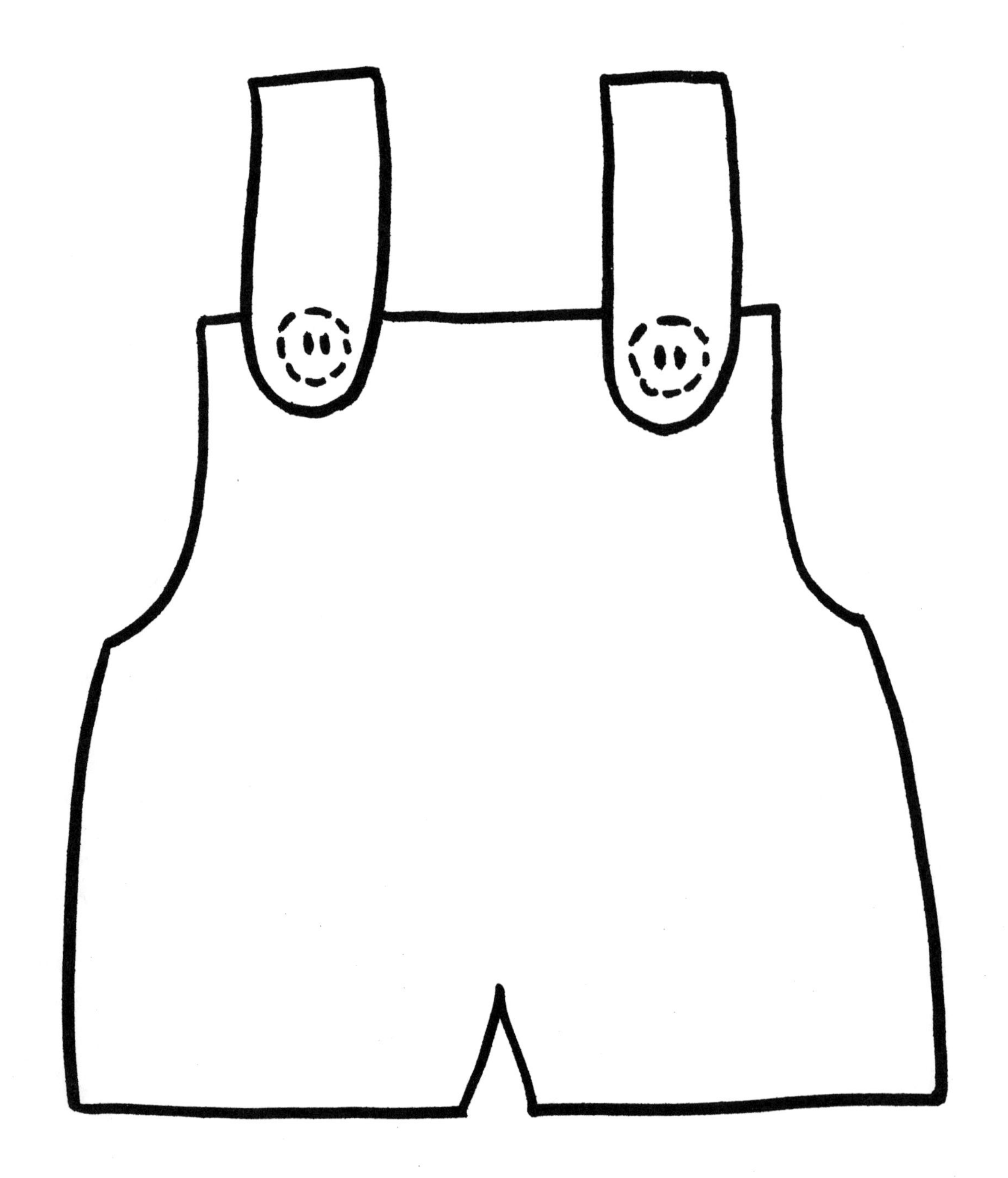

PIG

Materials
Construction paper:
pink for head, ears, and feet
orange for nose
Paper plate
Pink tempera paint
Pink or orange pipe cleaner
Scissors, glue, crayons or markers

Construction
1. Paint paper plates the day before pig is to be assembled. Let plates dry overnight.
2. Cut out all pieces.
3. Glue pig's head to front side of plate.
4. Glue four feet to back of bottom edge of plate. Use black crayon or marker to make hoof marks on feet.
5. Glue ears to each side of head and nose to lower half of face. Draw eyes just above nose. Make two little black marks for nostrils in middle of nose. Draw mouth just under nose.
6. Tape or staple pipe cleaner that has been curled to back side for tail.

Related Reading

Brown, Marc, and Krensky, Stephen. *Perfect Pigs: An Introduction to Manners.* Little, 1983

Galdone, Paul. *The Three Little Pigs.* Houghton Mifflin, 1984

McPhail, David. *Pig Pig Grows Up* and *Pig Pig Goes to Camp.* Dutton, 1980, 1983

Peck, Robert Newton. *Hamilton.* Little, 1976

Watson, Pauline. *Wriggles the Little Wishing Pig.* Houghton Mifflin, 1978

White, E.B. *Charlotte's Web.* Harper & Row, 1980

POEMS: "This Little Pig Built a Spaceship" by Frederick Winsor
"The Pig" by Roland Young
"The Hare and the Pig" by L.J. Bridgman
"I Had a Little Pig" (Anonymous)

Story Starters

Read *Pig Pig Grows Up* and then discuss the difference between being a baby and being a child. "Write a story telling how you knew you weren't a baby anymore." "Do babies need more attention? Why?"

"How would you like to have a pig for a pet? Pretend that you have a pet pig and write a story about him or her."

Follow-Through Activities

Use the book *Perfect Pigs: An Introduction to Manners* to begin a unit on manners.

Students may have fun writing a poem about a pig. "Use rhyming words to write a silly poem about a pig."

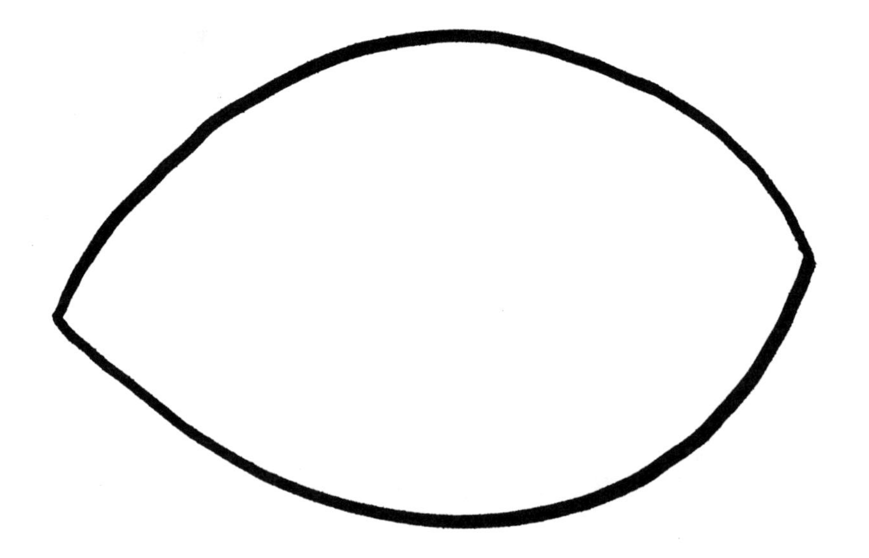

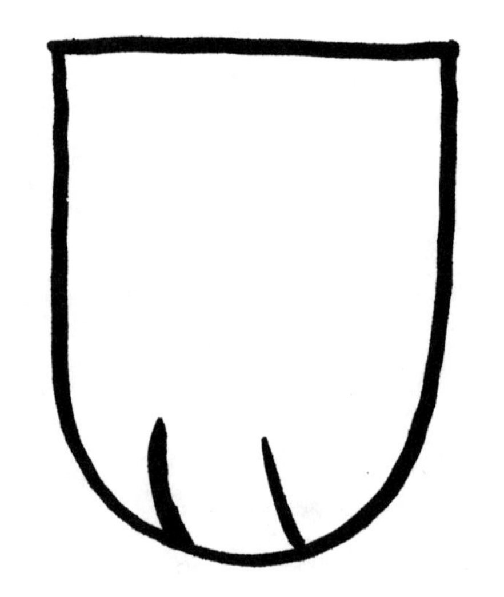

HIPPOPOTAMUS

Materials
Construction paper:
 brown for head and body
 pink or orange for mouth
 white scraps for teeth
Scissors, glue, crayons or markers, red chalk

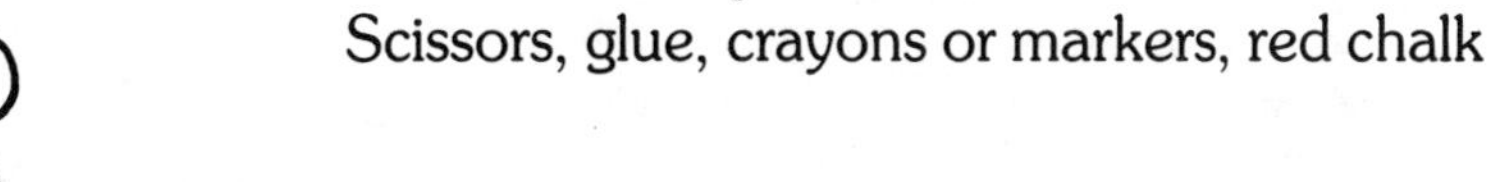

Construction
1. Cut out all pieces. Teeth can be cut freehand.
2. Glue mouth onto front of head, overlapping at least half of face.
3. Glue head to left side of body, overlapping a small portion of the mouth area. The placement of head at different angles will give each project its own personality. Let students be creative.
4. Use marker or crayon to draw mouth, nose, and eyes. Trace around feet.
5. Cut teeth from white scraps and glue under mouth line. Rub red chalk into cheeks.

Related Reading

Brown, Marcia. *How, Hippo!* Scribner, 1969
Boynton, Sandra. *Hippos Go Berserk.* Little, 1979
Mahy, Margaret. *The Boy Who Was Followed Home.* Watts, 1983
Marshall, James. *George and Martha* Series. Houghton Mifflin, 1972–1980
Thaler, Mike. *A Hippopotamus Ate the Teacher.* Avon, 1981
Waber, Bernard. *You Look Ridiculous Said the Rhinoceros to the Hippopotamus.* Houghton Mifflin, 1979
Weiss, Nicki. *Hank and Oogie.* Greenwillow, 1982
POEMS: "The Hippopotamus" by Jack Prelutsky
"Habits of the Hippopotamus" by Arthur Guiterman

Story Starters

"Write a story about how you think the hippopotamus got its name."

"Write a story describing the hippopotamus, using as many descriptive words as you can."

"Write a make-believe story about why you think the hippo has such a big grin."

Follow-Through Activities

Use *hippopotamus* as a special spelling word. Help students break the word down into parts.

Write the word *hippopotamus* on the board vertically. Ask students to help you think of words that begin with each letter of this word that could describe a hippo (example: H = huge, happy, husky). Students can write the word vertically on their papers and copy words down as the teacher writes them. Older students may enjoy doing this activity independently. Let them share their lists with everyone by making a classroom book for the learning center.

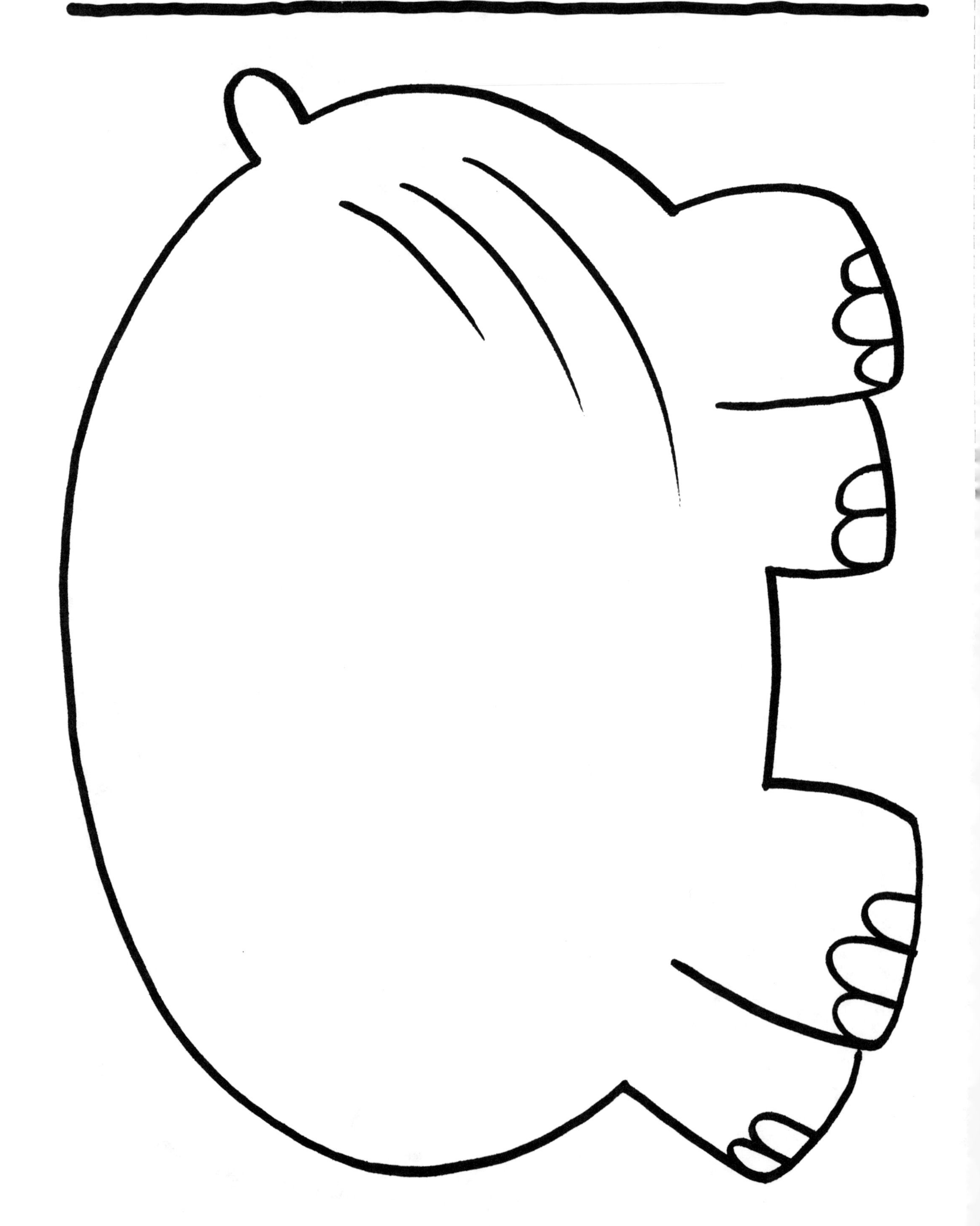

CHILDREN'S WRITING

Frogs

Frogs live under water.
They need to come up for air.
They are green too.
And they get new skin.
Some frogs have brown skin.
Frogs also eat insects
Carrie

BY Andrea
FROGS

Frogs eat flys. Once they
are born they stay under
water and they can breathe.
And then they eat and eat
and eat and become frogs.
Some frogs are ugly, but
some frogs are cute. The End

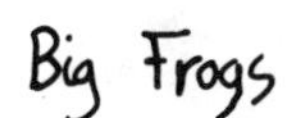

Big Frogs

frogs run away when they hear you.
They would be good basketball players.
They sometimes get air.
They jump around sometimes.
They jump up and get flies.
Some frogs are old.
We have fogs live in our pond.

CHILDREN'S WRITING

I wish I was a giraffe
because I would be so tall
I would not have to do my school work
I would move to Hawaii. If I lived in
a city I could look through the
tall windows I could see all the people.

The End Scott

I wish I was a giraffe because
my neck is long
and my neck can touch
the sky. I can see the sky
and I can touch the sky.

I wish I was a giraffe because
I could be tall as the pond.
I will live in Africa because
I get sun tan. I have spots on my
body and neck. I have horns
on my head. I will be a girl
giraffe and have babies. The end
Noelle

CHILDREN'S WRITING

My Dog Pee Wee
PeeWee rolls on her stomach.
She likes to run in the house.
She sleeps on the bench.
I Like to play with her.
She Likes me and I
like her.

My Dog Freckles
Freckles does silly thing
She growls at brothers Bill and
Joe. She runs out the door
when the door is open. She
Likes to play outside. She
digs in the sandbox.
Trish

My dog Nicky
My dog Nicky chases
kittens. He sleeps in a bed
in the garage. He is
black and white
He comes with me when
ride my bike. He's my
friend.

CHILDREN'S WRITING

I wish I was a mouse
because I wouldn't have to do
any work. But you would have to
find a place where I would go
to the bathroom. I wear lots of
earrings I could not swim or eat
because I couldn't reach.

Julie

Mandy

I wish I was a mouse
because I like cheese.
I hope my cat doesn't eat me
and my mom doesn't squish
me. The end.

A True Story
Some times there
are monkeys they
have pink faces.
Some times they itch
themselves and they
itch other monkeys.